She's ILL

By:

ASHLEY WOODS

Copyright © 2019 Ashley Woods

All rights reserved. No portion of this book may be reproduced in any form without permission from the publisher, except as permitted by U.S. copyright law. For permissions requests write to the publisher addressed

"Attention Permission Coordinator"
authorashleywoods@gmail.com

ISBN: 978-0-578-58355-6

Ordering Information: For information about special discounts available for bulk purchases, sales promotions, fund-raising and educational needs, contact the Author at the above email

DEDICATION

This book is dedicated to my sister, Jolynn & Terrell Bruce.

Sister, watching your battle with schizophrenia has been inspiring. Despite your struggles with enjoying life and motherhood, you still made the choice to have my nephews. I admire you for your strength and love.

Rell, you were the most honest and straight up person I've ever had the honor of knowing. Your memory and light continues to impact people to this day. Rest in peace.

Last but not least: to all the people suffering, silently or otherwise, from mental health issues: this book is for you. Read its pages and know that you are not alone.

FOREWORD

Damn, Dad.

As I review and make the final edits of this book, the very thing I've been dreading in the earlier chapters has happened. My father Samuel Zay-Zay passed away 9/11/2019. I'm broken right now, but I'm not defeated. I knew this day was coming, but there's no preparing for it. You see, we are challenged everyday and then just when you think things can't get worse-they do. It's okay though. Because of therapy, support, and self-awareness I'm able to deal with the situation a lot better.

My father's death has also given me clarity into some of his decision making and maybe the universe wanted me to know this before this book was completely done. My dad's pain, shame, and secrets were revealed and that's why he would depend on alcohol. I never took accountability of his kids and family back in Liberia and their feelings towards him for leaving and not coming back. The power he had over him. My dad had a lot of bad dreams growing up which felt real to him. He would argue and scream in his native language and move around a lot and fight. My mother and I just dealt with it. We never knew what to do. Dad, you're finally at peace. You're no longer suffering and, more importantly, you don't have any worries. I'm sorry I never asked you certain questions. I understand now you were doing what was best and protecting me from your trauma. This sometimes got the best of you. It's okay, I forgave you a long time ago and I love you dearly and wish that I could have been there for you.

INTRODUCTION

MY SISTER TRIED TO KILL ME

I know that you may think I'm joking or maybe even exaggerating but, unfortunately I'm not. This was my introduction to mental health. I remember being awoken from my nap by my sister. She wanted to play. I was ecstatic. My sister was seventeen years my senior and I wanted to do everything with her. I followed her upstairs to the 3rd floor. She said we would play a new game she saw her friends play with their sisters and brothers. I asked her the name to see if I already knew how to play and she said she forgot but it was like cops and robbers. Being an intelligent six year old I pretty much thought I had the concept down. So I happily said okay. My sister directed me to turnaround as she then proceeded to tie my hands behind my back. I was the bad guy & I was handcuffed. She then directed me to get in the tub which I noticed already was filled with water. I was confused because I was still in my clothes. I asked her if she was sure and she reassured me that it would be fun. I got into the tub and the water was cold. I remember her stuffing something in my mouth. I became scared but really couldn't do anything at that point because I was still handcuffed with my hands behind my back. She told me to wait real quick and went into the other room where she came back with a baseball bat. My eyes grew large; I was confused and didn't understand the game she was playing. She was talking to herself and swinging the bat back and forth. Crying, I closed my eyes but I could hear her mumbling.

Suddenly I remember hearing my mother call for me from downstairs. I immediately opened my eyes only to see my sister now charging at me swinging the bat in my direction. Crying I closed my eyes as I prepared myself to be hurt by someone I thought loved me. My mother saved me that day. I heard my mother scream *"What the fuck are you doing"* as she removed the bat from my sister hands. My sister said she was sorry and that she was only playing with me. The game didn't feel like a game anymore to me. I remember being taken out of the tub and told to change my clothes. Next thing I knew, we were riding in the back of a cop car. The cops and my mother were conversing but I couldn't process anything at the moment. I was in a daze recalling the events that just happened. All I knew was that my sister wasn't acting normal. After that incident, everything was a blur.

I remember us visiting my sister several days later at a facility. My sister had a green scrub set on. There were a lot of women with the same uniform on as my sister. I thought my sister would be in jail for what she tried to do to me. This place had televisions, a game room and the people appeared to be free. She eventually came home but did not stay with us. My mother or nobody else ever talked about it, it's like it never happened. I even wanted to forget about it. My sister often apologized over the next few years. As I grew older I discovered she had schizophrenia. She had a nervous breakdown the night of her prom and was never the same after that. She required medication to help keep her stable. Moving forward, my sister got the help she needed and began to act less erratically. Our relationship became solid and I looked forward to staying with her and her boyfriend on the weekends.

Chapter 1

I was diagnosed with PTSD in 2012. Through various testing and conversations with doctors, it is believed that my trauma started in childhood and that my time in the military added to it. A lot of these experiences weren't normal but my parents swept it under the rug. A lot of issues within my family weren't talked about; I was taught to forget it. Yet things continued happening and past experience resurfaced. I know now that I'm not the only one with these experiences. Old memories come back, ones that leave my mind consumed with a tsunami of unanswered questions. Thoughts that I don't want to deal with tend to linger, despite how hard I try to block them out. I never understood and still don't even today why we aren't taught to talk about our issues. How can anybody overcome a tragedy; or traumatic experience if they don't acknowledge it? That's why today some people don't take mental health seriously. For me abnormal acts were normalized like in most households and when you're a child adult's think that your memory is short.

My memory could not be short because I had to deal with parents that provided physically but neglected me in many other areas. Living through my father's infidelity, my mother being shot, my sister starting fires, my sister jumping out apartment windows, being come onto by one of my cousins' father, my cousin moving in and robbing me when I asked him to move out. I soon discovered once enrolled in the military that I had a heart that couldn't handle the requirements to stay in long term. I suffered from seizures and was hospitalized over 50 times including a mild stroke at 26 while living in Atlanta. I had nobody by my side during that time. I thought making more money would cure it all. Nope! Money became the band aid to hide the pain, the abandonment I felt, and my lack of support.

6 figures ain't do right by me because I wasn't right mentally. I gambled over 80k, I brought material items, and did things for people that wouldn't jump for me at all. I still had a void! I still was broken!

Acknowledge, Accept, and Absorb. I am 34 years young and I am just now figuring things out. In 2017 I was so hurt and unaccepting of my diagnosis. I tried to commit suicide by driving my car off the bridge by the zoo in Philadelphia. God wouldn't allow it to happen. It was after that I decided to check myself into a facility. I was slowly bouncing back through the help of my school mate named Terrell. Terrell was helping me manage my property better, helping me manage my finances better and sadly he was murdered. I felt broken again. I felt like I would not ever get out of the hole I dug myself into. I had to file for bankruptcy. In the midst of all the chaos I was able to publish a children's book. I sold over 700 copies and it was something even today I'm very proud of.

You would think working in Afghanistan for 2 years I would be mentally tough. While in Afghanistan encountering bombs and all types of stuff in the civilian contracting world just kept me distracted from what I've been running from. Each thing that was happening to me continued to pile. The one joy I did still have was making people laugh which was an outlet for me.

The moment I started to take my mental health seriously the better I started to understand me and love me more. I learned to embrace my mental health diagnosis. I used to be embarrassed; but I realized my pride did me no favors but only hindered me. If you're experiencing any symptoms like I did the 3 steps which has been helpful for me is:

Acknowledge that you have a problem! It's okay not to be okay. What's not okay is refusing to get the help that you need. You owe it to yourself to live the life you want to live despite your diagnosis. Your condition doesn't define you, but how you let it affect you *will*. Yes for some people the journey is rougher than others, but your mind is the most powerful thing you have. What you affirm is what you'll attract. I had a habit of thinking negatively and that's what would happen to negative things. I hung around with bad energy. I became that energy. When you have a mental health diagnosis you can't compile it with other negative things, or people, or places. You have to protect your energy at all times. Depression and anxiety are experienced by a vast number of people. It's just that some people are ashamed to admit it. When you acknowledge what you have going on you take back your power. Don't suppress your power by being ashamed.

Accept who you are and deal with it accordingly. After you acknowledge you must accept that the diagnosis is now a part of you. It doesn't define you but it is still a part of who you are. Once you can accept your diagnosis you will be willing to adapt. Adapting allows you to see the changes that need to happen so that your mental health doesn't overwhelm you. If we let things untreated for too long we jeopardize ruining a solution like I did when I tried to commit suicide. I almost destroyed myself and I thank God every day that I didn't.

Absorb the help that's out there. Whether it's from a therapist, in a group setting, taking prescribed medication, dedicated time for yourself or whatever it may be. Don't rob yourself! Save yourself because no one else will do it for you. You have to be your best advocate. Getting help is equivalent to standing up for yourself. Sometimes we go through multiple treatments to find that right one but never give up. There's someone out here that needs you. There's someone who believes in you. There's someone who loves you whether you see it or not. I believe everyone has something to live for and fight for outside of themselves. Now that we have an understanding on the importance of Acknowledge, Accept and Absorb, let's talk about talking.

My parents didn't talk to me about the things that happened in my life and, as a result, I didn't talk about them either. Talking is like medicine. You don't talk to any and everybody but talk to a person or professional that you will feel comfortable with. With people not knowing the indicators in children or adults regarding mental health, if you have kids make it your business to talk about everything with them. Allow that dialogue to happen whether the conversation is comfortable or not. If I didn't cry or get angry then it was assumed that I was okay. I had behavior issues in school. I disobeyed my parents and I kept conversation to a minimum. Still nobody wondered why, or, they just said, "She's spoiled." Nobody asked me how school was, or what I learned. Nobody came to my basketball or baseball games. I became introverted and accustomed to being alone. People tend not to disclose their problems or thoughts because of judgement. I was always concerned with how people would look at me or what they would think because I was taught to look at having problems as being weak. My pride kept me quiet and I wish it hadn't. You don't need to tell everyone everything, but you have to get negative thoughts out of your head or they will get the best of you.

Keep a journal and write down everything good or bad that happens to you. Identify through rereading your journal entries the things you've done that make you feel better. Look for patterns within the journal to help find your happy place. My happy places are when I'm writing, playing sports or swimming. My mind is clear when I'm doing these things. When I write I feel like it's a personal conversation between myself and my thoughts. This has helped me because I'm not keeping my thoughts bottled up which eventually will become anger if not released. There are so many ways to express yourself and, if you want to have a peace of mind, you have to work for it.

I have PTSD (Post-*traumatic Stress Disorder*). This is a disorder where people have difficulty recovering after experiencing or witnessing a terrifying event. Episodes tend to last long and certain experiences trigger the very event that was traumatizing. I had nightmares. I have guilt. I was once afraid of people like my sister in fear they would try to hurt me. I delayed getting the help I needed in order to avoid taking medicine. I had seen how dependent my sister's life was on medication; after the birth of her second child and having been without her medication for such a long amount of time, she relapsed and never bounced back to being as highly functioning as she was before. When her medication was working it was like she didn't have a condition. So one day her combination of meds just stopped working for her. I was afraid of doctors exploring to find what works best for me. I was afraid to become dependent on medicine. I was prescribed medication to help with my nightmares as well as to relax me, but I didn't like how they made me feel. So, I stopped taking it.

I made it my business after being in denial and stubborn to seek the help that I needed through therapy. Once I found the right therapist, life became better for me. The more I went, I became less ashamed of how I felt and more comfortable sharing my story. What's crazy is that I still cry when I talk about my past because I really had no support. I didn't feel the love and nothing felt genuine. My whole life has been the motto, "Get over it". For years I was damaged. I found myself fighting battles for other people when I couldn't even fight my own. I served a country who didn't support mental health like they should. I know for someone reading this book that the days seem consistently dark but there's always a light at the end of the tunnel. I had a handful of people who believed in me. All I want now is to be able to use my experiences to help someone else. You are not alone! You are worthy of life!

Chapter 2

FORGIVENESS

Death. Rape. Abuse. School. Work. Money. Everyday living. Mental health can be triggered by all these things and more. When you are not who you need to be you make decisions based on the wrong version of yourself. I found myself in bad relationships after bad relationships because I didn't hold the ones I loved to any sort of standard. I was so happy with some type of attachment or any form of love that I accepted anything, even if it wasn't what was best for me. I found myself dealing with other people who were damaged, and had baggage like myself. I thought that by fixing them, I might be able to somehow figure out a way to fix myself. This is not how it works. I can admit it was a time I was intimidated by a strong woman with her shit together thinking they would see things within me and be turned off or not give me a fair shot. Two damaged people can't fix each other; negative energy will only affect you negatively. So please if you don't listen to anything else listen to this. Be mindful of your circle; of who you love and who you consistently interact and surround yourself with. Everyone can take head of the previous warning, but for those of us who suffer from mental health this especially rings true. Allowing just anyone into your circle who may play games with your mind can hurt you and stunt your growth with managing your illness. I compromise myself. I sacrificed myself for people who did not have my best interest at heart.

I was diagnosed in 2012 and it took 5 years for me to begin to get the help that I needed. Though I am still a work in progress, I have found my purpose. My purpose is to let those reading this book know that it will be okay. Even if you don't think it will. Something that I strongly believe is that before you can take care of someone else, you have to take care of yourself. This is the lesson I had the hardest time trying to figure out. I have been a lot of things for people that I haven't been to myself. I learned how to depend on myself. I learned how to love myself. I learned how to support myself. I was none of that to myself because I was always hard on myself and doubting myself while running away from what hurt me. I really was out here caring about and loving people more than my own damn self and that's not cool. Not one bit. When I started loving both the good and the bad within me I was then able to forgive the hurt my parents caused me. I was finally able to understand that my parents made mistakes but they loved me, and they probably thought what they were doing was the best. I forgave them for not being there for me; I forgave my dad's alcoholism as well as the verbal and physical abuse that I had to endure. I didn't do it for him-I did it for me. I started being proud of myself. I had so many accomplishments to be proud of, such as being an author, serving my country, obtaining my degree in human resource management, and for being a business owner. I've donated to many causes, I've traveled; I've been a constant shoulder to lean and cry on for so many people and I'm proud of that. I had to understand that I was a beautiful person inside out and no disorder can limit me. You have to be everything for you before you can be anything to anybody else.

To anybody who loved me while I was still finding myself-I apologize and I appreciate you. The steps that have helped me to forgive and ask for forgiveness are listed below.

1. Pray not for what you want, but for what you are willing to work for. We have a tendency to ask

God for things that we're not ready or prepared for mentally. You have to be real and honest with both Him and yourself.

2. Forgive those who have hurt or disappointed you. Squash any beef or hate for people because it's too much energy and power that could be going towards bettering yourself.

3. Make time for yourself. Take a block of time in your day and make it about self-care. Whether it's a walk in the park, getting your hair done, exercising, or anything else you enjoy-is so important to make time to make yourself happy. I find this useful because it allows me to understand that even though I'm busy and have people I need to care for, finding time for self-care allows me to decrease stress and tension in my life.

4. Affirmations. As much as I was against this when I first started therapy, both my brand manager, and my publisher advocates for positive affirmations. I never did it consistently but once I started my mind started to train itself to think more positively. I was always so quick to think the worst of myself and positive affirmations helped me to alleviate my self-doubt and negative thinking.

5. Be okay with knowing that sometimes things won't be okay. When you're having a bad day, try to tell the people most important to you. Whether you need their comfort or you just need space, communication is key. Communication is important because although people might be sympathetic or even empathetic to your condition they still don't understand what you go through. Communicating with them is a proactive way of

having them aware of your feelings and respecting your space. When you feel a bad day coming, wrap yourself up in love, affirmations, and prayer. Remember to breathe and let yourself relax.

Remember diagnoses, disorders, and conditions are going to always be around but you will not. It's better to think about management versus wanting to get rid of it. We have to make the best out of who we are and if we want more out of ourselves we have to do more, be more! Your problems are not going to go away because you ask them to, they will when you find solutions and take action.

Do I still struggle with depression at times? Yes. I have things I have to do to make sure I don't allow my depression to spiral out of control or allow my mind to take me places mentally where I don't need to be. I suggest a plan of action for when the negative thoughts arise for you also. When you are feeling low, you need to do something to balance out your emotions. Review the 3 A's previously discussed during difficult times. Mental illness is a dangerous game if not taken seriously and you need to stay on top of it. I had to learn the hard way that my mind is the strongest part of my body. If you allow your mind to get the best of you, nobody will remember your intentions or your heart. They will only remember your negative actions. It's been a lot of times that my heart has been in the right place and my intentions have been genuine but my actions showed something different.

Think of solutions more than you think of your problems. The energy we invest in what's wrong in life or what we don't have or who don't love or support us takes away from the energy and effort in making a plan to execute our problems.

Chapter 3

There are a lot of undiagnosed people in the world. This is because we, as a society, allow our peers' views on mental health to deter us from being honest with ourselves about our struggles. Don't be ashamed for being different. You were custom built and you have to take some extra steps to make life work for you. You are a gift, you are talented, you are stronger than what you give yourself credit for. Let's stop limiting ourselves and start pushing ourselves everyday to manage whatever we are going through. If you struggle with mental health I am with you; I stand with you. I applaud you and I pray for you to overcome anything that has hurt you, set you back, or made you feel a type of way about yourself. A diagnosis doesn't dictate your character. Everyone has a bad day because none of us are excluded from the trials and tribulations of life itself. Don't ever allow someone else's success to make you think less of yourself. To the people that don't suffer from mental illness that decided to read this book, I thank you for opening up your mind into getting to know this world. I want you to know that the support that's needed from you if your loved one has a mental health diagnosis is very much needed. The last thing someone suffering from depression needs is absence from someone they love. Even if they distance themselves, just in some way show them you are there, you care, you may not have the answers but you are with them. When they come back around they will remember that and appreciate that, and some people might use that support as reinsurance the next time to let their guard down with you.

I've pushed a lot of people away because I was angry, afraid and confused on who I was and what was going to become of me. Repeat after me: ACKNOWLEDGE, ACCEPT, ABSORB! These 3 A's are going to get you where you need to be if you take each one of these seriously in your everyday life. The 3 A's aren't just for people suffering with mental health. This is where you can see your growth or lack thereof, because anybody can say they have a problem. The real challenge is facing it head on. Don't run away like I used to. When I signed up for the military that was me running away, when I moved to Georgia in September 2010 that was me running away, and when I went to work overseas in Afghanistan that was still me running away. Every problem I walked away from returned to me even bigger or just simply not resolved. It's just like people with addictions. They'll think, "I'm pissed, let me get a drink." Okay now they're drunk, and the problem is still there. It is actually now heightened due to the alcohol consumption. So don't just acknowledge that you have an issue, accept who you are, and absorb what's needed to be the best version of yourself. This process is not easy and it takes time.

You are your biggest critic. To truly deal with your mental health issues you must be honest with yourself. You can't be focused on how embarrassing or uncomfortable you feel because you'll need to stay focused. I was told in every phase of your life you have to get comfortable with being uncomfortable. Writing this book was uncomfortable for me in the beginning but then it became therapeutic. I absorbed that by sharing my story it has helped me in the process because it helps someone else. My journey hasn't been in vain. It has allowed me to grow mentally and embrace my flaws. Please do not allow society, peers, family or friends to make you feel bad about who you are or what you struggle with. You have to get selfish when dealing with anxiety or depression. It's a personal battle that needs your full undivided attention so you can get to the bottom of what you need to do to not be a victim. The victim mentality will get you nowhere; yeah you may have a few people feel sorry for you but that's about it. In all actuality it does nothing for us but allow us to soak in the pain of our past and halt our future. I once was a victim but only when I didn't know how to handle my mood swings. I displayed actions that were questionable. When I was around someone who called it out; I defended myself with excuses. That gets tiring and old real fast and it solves nothing. All I was doing was repeating things in my life but not really coming up with a plan and solutions to handle it. The bottom line: I wasn't growing from my past and would only talk about my problems when I felt threatened. Me writing this book is a testament to how far I've come in sharing my story without having to be forced into it. I'm not attempting to become the face of the mental health community, but if this journey leads to people following my lead, so be it. Out of all the things I do God has let me know that this is my purpose.

When you get out of your head you will get out of your way. I spent more time in my head with negative thoughts than I did with positive ones. I dwelled too much on things only to discover that things were out of my control. People are dealing with pain and questioning things that are simply not in their control. We have a lot to deal with in life so don't add on any unnecessary burdens upon yourself. I'm gonna say it again: **GET OUT YOUR HEAD**. You are holding yourself back. You are only going to go as far as you mentally allow yourself to. What you think will become good or bad. Make it a priority to surround yourself with good energy and speak things into existence. The power is within you. Nothing beats negativity like results.

When you have a problem and you find a way to solve it, that's one of the best feelings in the world.

When my friend Rell died it took the air out of me! The fact that an amazing man was senselessly murdered really broke my spirit. He was trying to make sure that I saw myself past my troubles. While mourning his death, I almost allowed it to make me give up on everything we were working on. I had to take all the pain; heartache and anger and turn it around to make him proud. I remember graduating from Chestnut Hill College a little over four months after his death and thinking-I got this. I put his shirt on my chair at graduation and made sure he was with me every step of the way. I took all those negative thoughts and I shoved them somewhere just not in my head and personal space, and I began to heal again. There are going to be moments that test you, try you, and flat out break you down. But they don't have to define you. Those very moments that hurt you can be the very problems that help you.. A problem is only a problem if it remains unsolved. Life is an ongoing test and nobody is perfect. Show me someone who has a 4.0 GPA when it comes to life.

Chapter 4

SOCIAL MEDIA

People everywhere-from young teenagers to older adults-have to stop allowing social media to affect them. People are getting themselves worked up about people behind screens who are not even being honest with themselves. What I discovered with social media is it's going to be whatever you allow it to be. You have control over who you follow, who you allow to follow you, and who you respond to. So if you've got that much power-why let things affect us so much? A person can have all the money in the world and might be the most miserable person in this world. Don't allow social media to make you think that your life is not amounting to anything just because your life is not following someone's else's timeline. Social media has played a significant role in the lives of children, teens, and adults. People look to these different social media platforms for information, trends, relevance, validation from the unknown; or from people they don't know. This can lead to anxiety or add to whatever you have going on if you allow it to. Just like you can control who you're around, you can control who you follow.

Who and what inspires you? When you find that out it will play a key part in what moves you. I have numerous things that inspire me. My sister inspires me because she can't live the life she once did but she's happy in her own skin. My sister didn't let that stop her from continuously smiling. My best friend, Shawna, who, although we had our bumps in the road, never allowed our battles to blind her to the person I was inside. Stephanie: a woman that was hurt and scorned by tragedy I couldn't understand, yet still found a way to love me despite everything going on in her life. Rell: you look at me as Ashley; the person nothing more nothing less and I will forever be inspired by your gift of giving (R.I.P). Rell gave people hope, time, and his word and stood by it. These 4 people are people that no matter what has inspired me while allowing me to be who I am.

Sports and movies are both loves of mine. When I think about inspirational people I think of Kevin Love and Brandon Marshall. The ability they've shown to speak out and use their platform as athletes is respected and appreciated. Money can't change your mental health. Men don't express themselves enough and with mental health being so stigmatized by millions their bravery and willingness to help others is very dope and I appreciate that. Taraji P. Henson and Jennifer Lewis are two African American women who opened up about depression and anxiety. Though they are both celebrities they are humans also and have their own battles. What you have and what you go through are two different things. You cannot look at someone else's life and allow yourself to think they can't go through anything. $1 in your account or 1 million or more doesn't cure all of your problems. We have to stop allowing others hard work and apparent blessings to dictate whether we feel like they have issues are not.

Some of the reasons we lose control of our anxiety or depression is from our emotions. We get inside our own heads and then after that the emotions take over. If we are not in control of our thoughts we damn sure cannot be in control of our emotions. I allowed my emotions to get the best of me plenty of times. My emotions were at their worst when I tried to commit suicide. I was so vulnerable. I was so hurt. I was lost as to why certain things were happening. The questions that continuously played in my mind were; how would I come out of this? Was life really worth living? I really disappointed myself.

At that moment when I planned suicide I didn't think of all the pain I would cause my loved ones. Suicide is no joke and is a huge part of why I was driven to write this book. I'm starting my journey as a mental health advocate in order to wrap my words around those who need comfort. There is a solution for every problem. God wouldn't allow me to drive off that bridge and I am so thankful he didn't. When I attempted suicide I had money in my account, new opportunities to travel overseas and make 6 figures, and plenty of experience to make money at home so money wasn't the issue. My inability to love myself and running from all my problems because I never learned how to deal with them were some of the reasons. I allowed my feelings to be so hurt that I felt hopeless, useless, and just didn't feel important. It wouldn't matter to anyone if I was no longer here, I thought. My emotions led me to feel defeated and because of that I almost made one of the biggest mistakes. At the end of the day, how could I rest peacefully if I committed suicide? I would have left so many people wondering what they could have done better. My parents probably would have blamed themselves. Questions left unanswered; like why? We ask questions when people die of illness murder or by accident, so imagine a person connected to someone who commits suicide the questions they would be asking themselves.

Life is about chances and choices, we have a chance everyday we are blessed to be here to make choices to change our lives. Sometimes choices come with sacrifice and doing things we don't want to do at times but it's a part of growth. Mental health is merely a diagnosis and we have to allow it to be just that. It doesn't define you unless you let it. It may at times dictate how you feel but it doesn't change who you are at heart. Make it a habit to learn how to control your emotions. Limit your negative thoughts. Find ways to make you smile. Do what you need to do to add substance to your life. Be productive. Don't fall into the mindset of not wanting emotions just fall in love with knowing how to handle them.

One of the best things that happened to me was being deployed with the National Guard during Hurricane Katrina in Louisiana. I was 20 during this time but the memories forever remain with me. Whenever I feel like I have a lot to complain about I reflect back to that time and empathizes with the victims and survivors. One day people were going about their daily routine and the next moment not having a home. Dealing with missing loved ones with no pictures and important documents gone and only being left with just memories. I've seen the pain and defeat in people's eyes when they had just lost everything. This allowed me the ability to see that I had the control to help myself. So now when I start to complain I realize that when I get out my way I can resolve things. When I do get down and mentally drained I think about the Hurricane Katrina victims because they didn't have the same choices in that moment that I still do. Their resources drowned along with their loved ones and their homes.

See when you're consumed with so much you lose sight of things and sometimes you have to put life into perspective. Work, school, and home can be stressful and overwhelming. We have to find that line that we are not going to cross because on the other side is a dark side and it puts us in a place where we stop living and we are only existing. When you only exist that's when the question creeps up. For example, we have plenty of people who wake up thinking, "Damn, I have to work to pay the bills, just to go back to work again. I have no life. You really do have a life but you have to look at it differently. A good example of this was when I was working at a job I knew I had no potential to grow. I knew how much money I could make with the job was limited and it wasn't enough. Instead of me becoming frustrated and quitting and left starting completely over, I began to pay attention. Through me observing all my coworkers I discovered everyone liked snacking at work. I went to Costco and stocked up on snacks. I then resold them and made $250 extra dollars a week. I was able to pay off tickets, pay down some bills so that when I got paid from my job I was finally able to start saving. There are plenty of ways to look at things, but we can't allow ourselves to become depressed about what we don't have. We have to learn how to cherish the gifts we've been given.

A myth I hate about mental illness is the belief that it has a look to it. The most ignorant line to me is "she got all that going for herself. I wouldn't think nothing was wrong with her". What do materialistic things have to do with mental illness? Like come on who comes up with this shit! I have been to Dubai 20 plus times and various other countries; I've seen 90k in my account; I had a 70K car, luxury apartments, a home I owned, and worn the latest designer clothing, but my mental health did not give two shits about that. I lost it all because I was mentally struggling with an illness and I was in denial about it. I started gambling my money away and isolating myself and was not handling business. A person can appear to have it all through other eyes and you don't even know that they are one step from losing it. I would trade all of that for peace of mind.. You can't purchase your way out of depression, I tried. God sees everything you can't outrun your outcome. Money doesn't buy happiness, it buys material items. Your bank account can't account for your well-being. So to the people that doesn't think that man who's on that block that sells drugs, and pop bottles in the club and get all the women he wants don't have any issues you have a lot to learn. People will cover what they want to hide and hide what they don't want people to know. We trick our minds into believing it's for our best interest but it's hurting us more by not having the ability to be ourselves. I went years not being who I truly was. I was trying to fit in, hide my flaws and to seem normal like everyone else. Nowadays, I don't know what normal is even like-and I don't care to know. I don't wish to fit in or be like everyone else. I am comfortable with who I am and I hope you are with yourself as well. Trends end at some point of time and all of them are not meant to be followed but being yourself willed never go out of style.

You couldn't have told me a few years ago I would be writing a self-help book trying to help others so that they'll know they aren't alone. To be honest, this book will probably help me more than I'll ever know. The ability to share my story is helping me get the closure I needed to move forward in life. Due to my parents' health, I can't talk to them about the things that have hurt me and ate up at me to the point where I signed up for the military at age 16. I've always found a way to run away from my problems, because I was afraid of dealing with them and the things that came along with it. A lot of people say they prefer the truth; well, I didn't. I wasn't ready to handle it. This book is so much more than a story about me. It's about people coming together and respecting one another. Put mental illness aside or any other thing you are battling with, respect is where it all starts. People are only going to understand but so much about you and your journey, your struggles, some might relate or have similar situations but no matter what everyone lens on life is different. We view things differently and we feel things differently. Face it, you have some people that see mental illness as a weakness, or a cry for help, or some bullshit doctors made up- and yes people lie and may abuse the system but that doesn't represent everyone.

Chapter 5

TRAVELING

If you haven't traveled please do so now! Traveling is one of the most exhilarating hobbies I have experienced. Whether it's to another state or another country, don't underestimate what a change of scenery can do for you. It's been a healthy outlet to be able to regroup, refocus and to take a break from Philly. I always feel rehabilitated and have new energy when I can get away from my everyday life. Traveling allows me to be able to think and analyze with a clearer mind. Sometimes when you're home and indulgent in your everyday lifestyle, you are not as attentive to some areas of your life as you should be. You have to make time for yourself and if you think you can't afford to get on a plane, try a train, bus, or a car ride. Always try to go somewhere new to learn new things and experience that city culture and what they have to offer. Take pictures and create memories.

A great suggestion is to get a book. This book will only be used to capture the new places you explore. Make notes to yourself about your time there. Include in your book anything pertaining to what you did. Favorites foods you ate, and anything and everything else that made that trip memorable. When you are feeling down, get your book out and just reflect on you living life. Everytime I'm doing something that I never thought I could do, it drives me to do even more. I never thought I would get on a plane. I never saw myself traveling anywhere outside of PA, DE, NJ, or NY. I always thought people wouldn't get who I was and what I was into. The amazing thing about it all I discovered is when you travel you're not alone. Someone else is traveling to that state or country for the first time also which is very similar to this battle with mental health; you're never alone!

Chapter 6

BULLYING

One thing I would like to address is the emotional trauma children are going through with bullying. If you think they are not dealing with anxiety and depression you are not paying attention. Television, video games, social media, peers, YouTube and their household has put certain beliefs and ideas in these children and young teen minds. This in turn places an immense amount of pressure on a child. Instead of getting to know people for who they are and how they make you feel, children are making decisions based on looks, popularity, assumed financial status, and social status. If you don't look like everyone else something is wrong with you, your weight, your sneakers, the way you dress, the way you talk, how your parents may look. It's really sad that a lot of these educational institutions especially in poverty stricken neighborhoods children are robbed out of their childhood. They are making decisions based on emotions, feelings, and fear of the unknown to be accepted by their peers.

Youth are taking things into their own hands. Parents, schools, teachers and people are not taking into account the things children are going through. Young boys are being taught that it's weak for a boy to cry; to never snitch; always fight their own battles. So why would young men in turn speak up when in trouble? How can we tell a child something is not that bad based on our own perspective? How can we tell a child that their fears are not warranted or real? We don't like to be judged. We don't like to be hit. We don't like to be talked about. So why would it be any different for a child who experienced these things? All of us are not built with certain characteristics and we can't dictate what a child should be like or be able to handle based on our personal perceptions and stereotypes. How can a child...when they are not living in a household that is allowing them to act like children behave like a child? Some children are caring for their siblings more than they should. A lot of children are constantly back and forth between parents and guardians homes. A lot of children do not have stable homes, balanced meals, clean clothes for school; yet we push them out into the world and assume they'll be ok. These children in turn are getting bullied or turned into the bully. Our kids are suffering with mental health just as much as adults.

My hopes are that one day the school system will start implementing classes talking about mental health, bullying and other important matters. With adults we have the mental capacity to understand that with bad days there may be light at the end of the tunnel. With children especially the ones committing suicide they might not have the mental capacity to see that. Imagine being in 4th or 5th grade and experiencing bullying wondering daily when will it end or if it's ever will end. Unfortunately, sometimes ending their life is the solution they come up with to end their problems. Adults sometimes don't have a handle on life so how can we expect a child or young teen too. I encourage you to get to know your child(ren). Encourage respect for others, courtesy, mannerism, your specific environment does not dictate teaching your child about respect and kindness. We are living in a time where kids are truly hurting other kids and not enough is being done about this ongoing epidemic.

Mental health has been knocking on our door. When do we answer the knock and face it head on. Hurt people hurt people. These kids are walking around with a lot happening in their lives and they are taking to replication video games, tv shows, or what they see at home to resolve their issues. No household is perfect, but collectively we all can do better.. We share hate more than we share love. That's why I'm standing up, because I look relatable, I am relatable and if we don't start talking we keep losing more and more babies. We can't be ashamed to tell our story and to be ourselves. We must become an example for children. I don't have children but I have nephews, cousins, god-kids, that look up to me. I can't just be comfortable showing them the good allowing them to think that rough days don't exist, how they can grow and learn how to navigate in this world if we don't be real with them. Some people want to protect their children but they are going to experience things outside our control one day and what will they have to reference when life gets tough for them. In a perfect world daddy wouldn't cry, mommy wouldn't struggle- but life isn't perfect.

We have children out here that are looking at our every move on social media. Children are observing how we interact with people, how we love, how we grieve, and how we handle adversity. If kids see us resort to the worst actions or feeling they are going to believe that's the action they need to take if they have a problem. We need to take a step back to reevaluate how we look at the word, "weak." Some people's definition is stunting their mental growth and affecting their children's growth. A man hitting a woman is weak to me, not a man crying. Weakness to me is the condition of one's mind. We cannot filtrate our minds with the belief that showing emotion and having feelings is weak. The focus is learning how to control it. It's up to the adults to teach children through our actions how to deal with their emotions and life struggles to prepare them for the real world.

Chapter 7

ROAD TO HEALING

When I sit back and think about how far I've come it does amaze me. I was so ashamed of myself because I didn;t understand who I was. It's so draining when you don't know who you are. It's a burden when you're around others that are so sure of themselves when you are not. The thing I learned is to not get caught up in others because what they portray versus what they really have going on is so different. We live in a world where people would rather look like they have it all together rather than actually have it together. I used to be one of those people. I let the high paying jobs, the designer clothes and sneakers, trips out of the country, speak for who I was. When it comes to your character no amount of money or material items can change that. I'm not gonna lie, it took me a while to find who I was. I discovered everything wasn't great and that's okay because I don't mind working on them. Along the way in my journey I realize I can come off selfish; in addition I was very inconsistent and my mood swings were like no other. This is where I had to step back and really understand who I was. I had to identify what I wanted out of life. I had to learn how I would deal with stress, depression and anxiety to continue moving forward in life. Through my pain and by being in denial I learned bad habits. I got so caught up with my issues I was dealing with internally, that it began to affect my relationships with people. Some people I never really gave a chance to be in my life or support me because my issues pushed them away. It was intentional. I'd like to take this time to apologize to anyone that genuinely was trying to be there for me who got the short end of the stick.

Truly finding yourself is an experience of its own. You have to be accepting of what you discover and not get mad. You have to adjust and basically try to recalibrate. When I accepted that I had issues with my mental health I was prescribed medicine. I am against that treatment, the thought of something altering my thinking or changing my mood scares me. Also, having a sister with schizophrenia who will never be the same anymore due to her medicinal issues haunts me. I still have memories of my sister when she was employed, had her own house, and was putting everything into raising my two eldest nephews. I feel like they've been robbed of those memories which make me against medication. I know it doesn't work like that in everybody's case but this has been my experience.

Talking has helped me a lot. When I replay situations it helps me to calm down and process things differently. I learned how to analyze things with a calm clear mind instead of acting off emotions that are deeply rooted in pain which makes my problems appear worse than what they are. If you need medicine please take it if that's what is best for your situation, I'm doing what's best for me and it comes with working 20 times harder because I don't take medicine! I have to immediately recognize when my mood is changing and either remove myself from my surroundings or think good thoughts to redirect my emotions. My moods are triggered by past trauma. Things will just set me off and people might not even know they are triggering me. That's where communication comes in if you want someone in your life and you love them you have to be honest with them. Allow people the choice if they want to deal with that part of you or not. You can't be mad if your mental health makes others nervous, timid, or not willing to deal with you on a certain level. People's views are different and you never know what they may have experienced which makes them afraid. Nowadays, as long as a person respects me as a person, I don't dwell on whether or not they really understand me. People that truly love you and want to be in your life will find a way to show their love and support. Again everything starts and ends with self-evaluation. You can't expect anybody to be true and loyal to you if you're not loyal to yourself.

Chapter 8

INCONSISTENCY

My inconsistency has me right where I should be, when I stop being inconsistent I will be further in life. My inconsistency stems from fear of being great. I wonder if I'll be able to handle it. Will I still be able to notice the change in people? Will I notice whose good or not? I was meant to deal and interact with people. My job on earth is to help people dealing with the same issues I'm dealing with. Writing this book I'm aware that I'm not coming to you perfect. I'm not coming to you like I have all the answers. I'm bringing you along on my journey and sharing the steps I took to get here. Don't allow people to make you feel like you need to have it all together to help someone out. You can learn from anybody-it all depends on how you look at and perceive things. I learn from children, the elderly, people that have been in prison, enemies, family, and friends. This book is not about flexing on anybody. This book is helping me in ways I never imagined. As I typed each word, I became stronger. I become the storyteller- someone who will not allow other people to tell my story through a cloudy lens.

When you find out who you are you will find peace. Every level brings a new devil but with that being said knowledge will always be power. No one can take you off your square if you are fully aware of who you are. I used to get so bent out of shape because someone might have said I was crazy; it only bothered me because I wasn't willing to accept my diagnosis. My character or heart doesn't change because I was diagnosed with PTSD. Words and people's opinion of me no longer hurt. I know who I am. I'm now aware that there are so many people who suffer from depression or have experienced it at some point in their life. There are people out here battling harder problems and situations than I am. I am thankful that I can do things such as writing a book. There are so many people who have taken their life before they had the chance to get the help that they needed. It's important to realize how precious life is. Who you surround yourself with is major. You are the energy you keep. You can't expect to deal with your problems if you're constantly around negative and miserable people. Surrounding yourself with positivity is key to maintaining good mental health.

When I changed my environment it was like I saved my own life. This life is always you versus you unless you're an athlete that's the only time it's competition. I can't be around people that constantly compete with each other, put down others, always have negative things to say.

Some people commit suicide without even taking their life figuratively but by mentally and physically drowning themselves in negativity and hatred. A mental health diagnosis doesn't make us inferior to the next person. Your gift, talent, character or heart has nothing to do with medical issues.

I love and support people so much that I tend to forget about myself. Learning how to be myself. Learning how to love myself helps me gain more control over my mental health. Trust me God will always expose who is for you. One of the major keys to mental health is seeing your progression. When you are depressed and dealing with anxiety you are not allowing yourself to see past the problem. When this happens you become stuck and the problem consumes you so much that it hinders you physically and emotionally on top of mentally. So make sure you are not knowingly putting yourself in a situation that's not good for you. I noticed I started to get into business and wanted to learn more so my interactions changed amongst people. I became more engaged with people doing more than me to learn and become inspired. When this happened the people who were always gossiping and being negative I started spending less time around. I spent a lot of time and money when I did not know who I was when I started to discover that I had to make choices and changes. I kept people around longer than I should. We have to be selfish at times to regain our sanity.

As I'm writing this book I'm dealing with the changing health issues with both of my parents. This has taken a toll on me because we didn't have the best relationship when I was growing up. I realized that despite our issues they've always done what they felt was best. These challenges have not stopped me from ensuring that my parents are properly cared for. I never wanted to put them in a nursing home-I want them to be together as long as possible. My father's health is rapidly declining and I don't know what to expect day to day. I find myself crying a lot. I even had to take time off from writing this book. I question my decision to become Power of Attorney often because it's a challenge.

With that being said I'm now aware that we all will go through various obstacles in life. There will always be things to shake up our world. We have to learn to try our best to recenter our mind back to positive thoughts so we can properly figure out solutions. If I just sit around and cry I'll continue putting the wrong energy into the universe and I'm shifting my blessings by stressing over things out of my control. We tend to look at adversity and question God. Adversities don't have to defeat you. Remember not to suffer in silence. When I was suffering in silence I almost died in hell.

Chapter 9

STEREOTYPES

Society has made it difficult for men to express themselves without being labeled as weak or a bitch. Brothers, there is no shame in sharing your pain, gains, and losses because sometimes anxiety and depression don't come from a form of pain or loss. It can also come from fame, attention, and money. Whether on the streets; working a 9 to 5; in prison; or unemployed life happens to them just like it does to us and their feelings cannot be overlooked. There are men who are single fathers and trying to provide; or a married man trying to hold his family down; or a man in between jobs; or with a criminal record which are all things that can be mentally draining. Men are faced with mountains of stress on their shoulders. Imagine the mental anguish for a man who grew up without a father or the ones who saw their father not properly love their mother. Being strong doesn't mean being emotionless. Research shows that this population experiences mental health issues quite frequently.

Right now I am facing a hard decision regarding my father's quality of life. Continue to fight or place him in hospice. My mind is racing. I'm filled with so much anger with the facility and myself. I find myself wanting to be alone but all that does is amplify my anger and I become overly emotional. I found myself not getting the things done that I know I need to. When my emotions begin to affect my peace that's when I know I have to reevaluate myself. What has helped me deal with the thought that I might not have my dad here by the time I'm done writing this book is our relationship today. My relationship with my father has strengthened over the years. My father started to soften his approach with me which showed me his caring side. It's so hard trying to hold it all together. But when I look at my book, especially the title, I think about the people I am trying to reach. The love I have for both myself and God have gotten me through the dark days. I pray your self-love and faith will do the same for you.

It's funny all the times I thought being alone would be best for me but that idle time wasn't good for me. Of course it's never anyone intent to think negatively but it's sometimes it's the only thought that comes to mind. I saved my own life by taking the step to self-discovery after accepting I had mental health issues. Every day I wake up I wake up with a purpose. I know that I belong in this world and God has an assignment for me. I used to think that making people laugh was my gift, but I use that as a shield to block out a lot of pain I was going through. The world can't be better unless we do better as people and embrace the uniqueness of one another. No matter who you are, you are somebody. And I hope that you find your purpose. I pray that you get through everything you're going through and that you are supported. I want you to know not to become discouraged if you fail at something. Keep trying. Failure is an opportunity for reinvention. It's okay to have to go back to the drawing board. Sometimes failure is the lesson that needs to be learned.

I opened up a new hair store in July 2018 and, due to the declining health of my parents coupled with a lack of support, I found myself closing it. I found myself supporting other people's dreams more than my own. I had a very bad habit of putting everyone before me because at that time I was still struggling with putting me first. I'm glad it happened because I believe God was showing me certain things and blindly I ignored the signs. That's the thing we all are warned in certain situations to walk away and not to do certain things but we do it anyway for whatever reason. As much as I wanted to point the finger at everyone; it was me who hurt the growth of my business.

The pain we feel sometimes is self-inflicted. If you don't value yourself or understand your self-worth how can others. The same respect given is the same that must be received. So yes, my business failed because of me. I failed to understand what I was taking on because I didn't devote the time nor do the required research. I didn't love what I had going on enough to put it first.

Don't get lost in your lover, your friends or family to the point you're not doing what's best for you because it can happen so easily and time goes by and you're in the mix but you really don't exist. I stopped hanging out with certain people and had to really look at where I wanted to be and started to go through a stretch where I was missing a certain atmosphere that was really unhealthy. Now I'm up here thinking why am I missing people that's not good for what I am trying to be, because of the lack of confidence I had in myself. The more I was alone the stronger I became, I didn't allow myself to be around to get caught back up, this was my test.

To be honest this is everyone's test in life breaking off from bad habits and the people you need to distance yourself from. It was nothing for me to gain but everything for me to lose. That's where I understand what happens and certain confrontations I had could have been avoided. I'm now aware that those fall outs were supposed to happen so I can be right here at this point writing this book and on this journey to be who exactly I needed to be to myself. When I think about it if I was around the same group of people I was with I wouldn't be doing the things I am doing now. I wouldn't have met the people I met and I damn sure wouldn't have gotten the blessings I've gotten. The best part of it all was finding myself and not getting lost.

Understand anything you do can affect your mental health. That's the purpose of me giving you little stories of my life, and my thinking at the time. The things you do in life represent where you are mentally. Look at that child that's really good in school but wants to fit in so the child starts hanging with kids that don't like school and who are rebellious. You look at the good student as to why he's hanging out with them not realizing this child feels alone and not good enough and this new crowd makes him feel accepted.

We got to build each other up, especially when we're doing well. All of this competition and envy are stopping people from giving kudos to those who deserve it. We have people of all ages doing amazing things but feeling not worthy because of the lack of support and togetherness our community has. I knew I was doing right because the things that started to happen to me after I changed my thinking. What was really encouraging were the things people said to me that saw me in that very environment. You never know what people see in you, and when they tell you it's a great feeling to know.

More and more, people have come to me expressing that they like me better doing what I'm doing now, which just confirms to me that I made the right decision. Be you, no matter what. Be around those that accept you for who you are, whether you are in a good or not-so-good place in life. We all have folks around us that are around us because it's more beneficial for them, or those friends and family that try to keep that connection with you just In case some dope things happen in your life. These are ways you can affect your own mental health by knowing these things and not doing anything about it. Shit is going to happen in life but try to handle and take care of the things you can control. That's what affects us is when things happen we can't control on top of things getting out of control we could control.

Don't be the person in therapy like me with a lot of self-inflicted wounds. That's why I am growing as a person, because I know what the hell is going on with me. I own that shit, and I'm handling it every day one step at a time. Don't own it and not do anything with it. That's another way of prolonging your healing.

Don't be afraid of taking a break from things to get yourself together. I had to break away to get my energy together. Even though your energy might not be great every day you have to work on it being good most days, and understanding when you're around great energy and when you're not. I notice if someone's energy is off and it used to affect me. Nowadays, I understand that I can't control the energy around me, but I can up and leave. You'd rather sit around bad energy and perhaps let it rub off on you instead of just removing yourself? I don't care if you're somewhere with a friend and they were your ride. Oh well, that's what Uber is for. This goes back to controlling what you can control and that's the best thing I've learned is the ability to walk away when something doesn't feel right. Don't wait for a bad situation to become worse.

I never thought I could be this vulnerable, but the more I talk about it the better it helps me and in the process it helps others. Allowing myself to build a relationship with God on my terms has helped me tremendously in my path. He knows I don't like the idea of medication and that I will lean on him during both the good times and the bad. I cannot attain any form of wealth if my health is not where it should be and when you think about health it's not just from a physical standpoint. I don't want to be rich with money but poor within my emotions. Let's not walk around looking good but never feeling good. Your mask might have to be on for certain situations, but how many times are you going to be able to put it on and take it off without hurting yourself in the process? We can post that caption. I don't look like what I have been through, and it's cute but if you are not whole within yourself , you're not hurting nobody but yourself.

We have to break the cycle of being in silence because we are worried about what others think. Those other people might just need you to break their own silence. I know life isn't perfect and never will be, but it doesn't mean you have to bury yourself in depression and anxiety alone. Talk about it, write about it, rap about it, do what's needed so that your days don't get so bad you feel like you're better off not being here.

Our mind is our power. It's the very thing that makes us who we are. Loving yourself has nothing to do with what you have, but it has everything to do with who you are. What you do, what you allow, what you condone, will show you how much you love yourself. Wake up every morning and look yourself in the mirror and tell yourself I love yourself, you gotta mean it though. Do things that make you happy, and if you have to do it alone then so be it, we have to stop feeling like we need others to be happy, to have a good time, to have peace. Your mental illness is about you and what you have going on, so your peace of mind should be about you as well.

Don't get caught up in relationships and friendships and get dependent on others to lift you up, turn up and make things fun for you, because the minute you go through something and they don't understand or realize it you'll even be more depressed or angry thinking you don't have no one when all actuality no one owes you anything especially not happiness.

You have to understand who you are and who you surround yourself with and who you will vent to, or if you will go to therapy. Conversations with friends are like therapy, they are just unlicensed and can tend to be biased or sugar coat things. Things I'm saying are easier said than done because when you are going through shit, you think about all this. The end goal is to be more aware of your actions so won't allow things or people to further affect your state of mind.

Chapter 10

GETTING HELP

I know that when I'm go through something that I can reach out to my therapist or talk to Ms. Cindy. My therapist helps me to find alternative ways of thinking and puts certain things into perspective for me. Ms. Cindy is the mother of some of my friends, ones that I've known for about ten years, and she knows my heart. She understands how I think and how to speak to me. Ms. Cindy doesn't sugar coat anything but I know when I talk to her it won't get back out, she will tell me if I was wrong and I just trust her. I have other people I can talk too also but I've learned to limit the amount of ears I vent to. Yes I am an open book and don't care about people knowing stuff but it's still people out here that will try to hurt you with their own information.

If you've ever thought that you might be better off if you left this earth, you're wrong! It's not the way to go. It's actually the easy way out of a problem that you really could have gotten through. Depending on your relationship with God and the people in your life, sometimes you'll think, "Damn. This is too much." I have two parents that are sick one of which is on his way out the door. I feel that if my father died my mom will not fight no more and will want to join him. Everyday it's a struggle to go to work, to run my business, to write this book because I'm hoping for the best but being realistic I know the end is near for my dad. As the power of attorney, I get the final say on a lot of things. It's scary and every decision I make for the doctors to save his life, I worry if I'm putting too much on him. I'm scared, I'm nervous, I rethink and overthink every decision I make driving myself up the wall. I'm bursting out of tears randomly. It's just a rollercoaster.

If I allowed my mind to revert back to how it was in 2017 and let the thoughts of killing myself resurface, who would that help. I now know that I will hurt people that love me and even worse leave my parents hanging because I came up on a tough patch in life and allow it to put me into shambles. No, I now know to lean on God and my support system during tough times because despite everything going on, I was meant to go through this. In this cold world we live in, I'm thankful for the time I had with my parents. That's my formula to lean on my support system and to think of all the reasons to be grateful. Suicide was once the answer but It's not anymore. If you've ever thought about it please reach out to someone or call the *National Suicide Prevention Lifeline 1-800-273-8255.* Although you might feel like it's the best solution, it isn't. It doesn't solve your problems. It merely perpetuates a cycle of hurt, with your pain being transferred onto someone else. You ending your life might lead to someone else's mental health depleting due to the grief and guilt. They will wonder why you did it and what they could have done to stop you. Life is not going to always be comfortable, but it's not always bad either and that's all you need to know.

What's so devastating about mental health issues is that they are extremely prevalent in a lot of households, yet it's still a subject that people refuse to talk about or acknowledge. I need you to really think about what you can do to help change the perception of people struggling with mental illness and making the conversation normal like everyone else. How can people be around people that talk about stealing, hurting others, scamming, and doing all types of things rather than make a big deal about the mental health crisis in our country? I don't get it. The people who are committing these crimes are probably suffering from it as well and don't know it. Do you think it's normal for a person to wake up and don't want nothing out of life, or not want to work for anything, but instead choose to rob and hurt people that get up and work hard for what they have? That's not normal but society picks and chooses what is cool to talk about and what's not. We all need to really sit back and think of ways to help ourselves first and then help each other. I refused to write this book and not be authentic.

The biggest thing about mental health is the judgment part of it all. When people think of mental health, they tend to automatically associate it with the word "crazy". Mental breakdowns happen every day across the world. You don't think that people being brought up in human trafficking or victims of abuse, molestation and assault are going to experience some form of anxiety or depression later on? A 15 year girl being pregnant, a son whose dad died, the list can go on, and at the end of the day things affect people differently. My relationship with my parents growing up and my relationship with my family, and certain encounters throughout my life has made it difficult over the years to maintain healthy relationships or friendships. I'm always worrying or paranoid about being done dirty or abandoned. When shit just keeps happening to you and you don't understand why-it can make you emotional. I love so hard for people because of the love I didn't know or receive growing. I've learned to give people the respect and love I wish to receive but in life it doesn't work like that.

I was fighting to survive in a world I felt like didn't like me or love me. I didn't understand I needed to love myself from top to bottom and having the mentality of "you're going to take me as I am or not all". I hid myself a lot because I feared people wouldn't deal with me if they knew my story. During my 20's I would be up at night thinking that dying might not be so bad. I was carrying the weight of trying to make my parents like me and be proud of me. I just always thought people dealt with based on what I was able to do for them. I showed what I can do first in a physical and materialistic form but never showed who I was. I was afraid of who I was, I was ashamed of who I was, I didn't love who I was. So just to think about all the people out here from kids to adults all across the world that struggle with so many different things it's just hard as shit out here. It will people who are suffering just like you that will judge you are looking down on you just because they can hide it better. Don't allow someone with a different struggle make you feel less of a person because they know how to suffer in silence. Mental health is not a joke and is as serious as cancer; we are all suffering from things so just because someone deals with it differently doesn't make anyone better than the other.

Chapter 11

MENTAL HEALTH DISORDERS

I feel like me coming out with this book was a perfect time to add to the conversation on mental illness. There are so many more mental health diagnoses other than anxiety. Some of the most common are, Depression, Anxiety, Schizophrenia, Bi-Polar, PTSD (Post-Traumatic-Stress-Disorder), Anorexia Nervosa, ADHD, Personality Disorder, Obsessive-Compulsive Disorders, Dissociative Disorder, Borderline Personality Disorder, Narcissistic Personality Disorder, and the list goes on. As you read the definitions of these disorders, you may recognize some of the symptoms of these conditions in either yourself or someone you know. This does not constitute a diagnosis, but rather, that those who experience mental health issues suffer in similar ways like the rest of us. The difference is that they are disorders that prevent individuals from functioning. So, if you or a loved one is experiencing some of these symptoms and you feel debilitated by them-go and talk to someone.

Depression (major depressive disorder or clinical depression): is a common but serious mood disorder. It causes severe symptoms that affect how you feel, think, and handle daily activities, such as sleeping, eating, or working. To be diagnosed with depression, the symptoms must be present for at least two weeks.

Anxiety Disorders: People that suffer from generalized anxiety disorder show excessive worry most days for at least 6 months, about a number of things such as personal health, work, social interactions, and everyday routine life circumstances. The fear and anxiety can cause significant problems in areas of their life, such as social interactions, school, and work.

Schizophrenia: is a long-term mental disorder of a type involving a breakdown in the relation between thought, emotion, and behavior, leading to faulty perception, inappropriate actions and feelings, withdrawal from reality and personal relationships into fantasy and delusion, and a sense of mental fragmentation.

Bipolar: a disorder associated with episodes of mood swings ranging from depressive lows to manic highs. This can come from a combination of genetics, environment, and altered brain structure and chemistry may play a role.

PTSD (Post Traumatic Stress Disorder): A disorder in which a person has difficulty recovering after experiencing or witnessing a terrifying event. The condition may last months or years, with triggers that can bring back memories of the trauma accompanied by intense emotional and physical reactions.

Anorexia Nervosa: people suffering from anorexia nervosa may see themselves as overweight, even when they are dangerously underweight. People with anorexia nervosa typically weigh themselves repeatedly, severely restrict the amount of food they eat, often exercise excessively, and/or may force themselves to vomit or use laxatives to lose weight. Anorexia nervosa has the highest mortality rate of any mental disorder, while man people with this disorder die from complications associated with starvation, others die of suicide.

ADHD (Attention-Deficit/Hyperactivity Disorder): is a brain disorder marked by an ongoing pattern of inattention and/or hyperactivity impulsivity that interferes with functioning or development.

OCD (Obsessive Compulsive Disorder): tendency towards excessive orderliness, perfectionism, and great attention to detail.

Dissociative Disorder: is a mental disorder that involves experiencing a disconnection and lack of continuity between thoughts, memories, surroundings, actions and identity. People suffering from this escape reality in ways that are involuntary and unhealthy and cause problems with functioning in everyday life.

Borderline Personality Disorder: is a mental illness marked by an ongoing pattern of varying moods, self-images, and behavior. These symptoms often result in impulsive actions and problems with relationships. People with borderline personality disorder may experience intense episodes of anger, depression, and anxiety that last from a few hours to days.

Narcissistic Personality Disorder: A disorder in which a person has an inflated sense of self-importance. This is more found commonly in men.

I listed the various mental health disorders because you may be able to identify similar characteristics in your behaviors or someone you know. This does not mean everyone is in need of a diagnosis. I will say that it proves that each one of us is one step or poor decision away from our life changing drastically. None of us are exempt from mental health issues.

One of the biggest misconceptions about mental health is that you cannot live a normal life. That's completely false. You'll have to learn to deal with life as it comes. It's important to find a reliable support system and the best thing you can do if you know you suffer from mental illness is to have your support system in tack the best you can and have your go to things to do that will ease your mind and bring you peace. That's why it is imperative we know ourselves first because identifying what makes us happy and what makes us breakdown can go a long way in our everyday life. When you commit to yourself you will help yourself.

Don't shield yourself from the world, don't shrink yourself for others, and don't be scared to show your scars. The more you're in tuned with yourself and living life the more you'll be able to handle problems as they come. So with the next situation you might still stress and be depressed about it but it might not last as long as another situation. That's a win; you have to look at all progressions in life as a win. Take for instance 3 years ago if your heart got broken and you may have keyed his car and bleached his clothes but this year your hearts broke and all you do is block him and his family from contacting you. That's progress. Loving someone will try your mental health like your mom straightening your edges in the kitchen with the blue magic grease telling you not to move and you can hear the sizzling sounds coming from your head. For the folks in the back that think mental health limits our greatness that's incorrect it enhances it. There are so many people out here doing great things. Inventors, athletes, artists, lawyers, parents, politicians, doctors, teachers, investors and the list can go on all may suffer from mental health. Some of the people who make sure that you're entertained are some of the millions of people who deal with mental illness. I didn't' want state names because it's not about the person status it's about the discrimination, the judgement, the lack of respect of those who suffer with mental health. This issue is so important but doesn't get talked about.

This book is not a cure. I don't have the answers to everything. It's merely a glimpse into my transformation and encouragement from me to you that you should not live in fear, shame, or doubt because of who you are. Don't walk around feeling like you have to hurt yourself to free yourself whether by drugs, alcohol, self-inflicted wounds, holding your pain in trying to fake like you're not going through anything. Anything you try to do that doesn't involve you dealing with it head on will always be a temporary fix and it will come back to you. I ran and ran and ran some more until I got hit hard with reality. You mean so much to this world and you don't even know it, there's somebody out there that would die to have your hand in life, there are countries out there that will swap out for your life, your opportunities, your healthcare, etc.

Pain, disappointments, rejections, hurt, triumph, tragedy, heartbreak will come, but it's all temporary depending on how you look at it. When you feel like damn stuff keeps happening to me you look yourself in the mirror and take accountability of what you need to change and do with the things you can control so that things won't come your way again. Look, I'm always going to be a work in progress. Every day brings a new set of troubles, but I approach it like a winner now, even if things don't pan out the way I expected. I look at the glass half full now. My negative thoughts are decreasing more and more. My positive thoughts increase more and more and I now depend on God first. Your faith is going to carry you to places money will never be able to. Wake up with a purpose because God woke you up on purpose so you were meant to do things mental illness or not. This is exactly why I called my book, *She's Ill.* it's a double meaning for me. Yes, I am suffering from a mental illness. But I am dope as hell! This is my journey from mental health to mental wealth. Finding myself will help me be rich, but helping others become comfortable being different will be my wealth.

This book is going to help me jump start my mental health advocacy. If I can help someone reach out for help a year sooner, a day sooner, an hour sooner it's a win across the board for themselves, their family and society. The more we get treated and the society gets educated the better we can heal and help those that need help without scrutiny or being belittled or demoralized. I was afraid of writing this book-I would get anxiety just thinking about how people would view it and whether or not I should write it because I'm not a licensed mental health professional. These were the various questions running through my head and then one day I was laying up thinking to myself about why I was doubting myself. This book is needed! I am a professional because I live it, I breathe it and it's my everyday life. I started to think about that family that lost someone to suicide and how they feel not being able to help that child or adult while they was here or not being able to catch signs to help. These thoughts made me more confident. Yeah to some, I will be a nobody. But this book is going to change and save lives. It is going to be the motivation that someone needs to start to help them.

I woke up in the middle of the night to write this book. That's all God and Him knowing what I need to do. I'm still trying to build my other business up but this book is a priority. This is me chasing my dream to not only be an author, but one that impacts and changes the lives of others.

Chapter 12

YOU'RE ILL

As I think about the mental health issues we are dealing with today, I wonder what the generations after us will face. There will be far more diagnosis and an entirely different level of issues. That's why it's important to get on top of this crisis while we can. **Acknowledge**, **Accept**, and **Absorb**-not just with mental illness, but with everything in life. If you are true to yourself, you will never do yourself wrong. Even amidst adversity and a cluttered mind, your foundation will remain intact. I did this exercise that helped me and I'm going to pass it along to you. I hope it helps.

Write down 5 situations you struggle with in your life.

What happened and why do you think you struggled?

Who/what groups were you hanging around at the time?

Who were you in a relationship with?

Who was your support system?

Where did you work?

What year was it and how old were you?

How long were you mad about it?

Detail your behavior, mood, and the part you played and didn't play in the situation

Then write down 5 things you did that were great and repeat the steps. These steps helped me tremendously. I was able to see during a certain period of my life I was around negative vibes and people who were not on my level. I was following others with materialistic possessions and drinking and I wasn't learning or evolving. I wasn't myself and I felt like I would be looked at crazy if I spoke about my problems. I can now see that some patterns of my behavior and mood changes affected me and made other situations happen or repeat themselves. When I got to the good side of the things I did great my circle of people changed and I started to travel with me and see the world. I actually hung with people that like to read. I'm a listener. I do audio or like to listen to people so I learned things like the stock market, politics, religion, my greatest accomplishments I actually shared with one other person or alone.

My support changed as my status changed. Everyone who was around when I could do something for them, but the minute my struggles came I couldn't go to those same people. I was able to acknowledge I had an anger issue, my mood changed when I didn't get my way, and I realized that wasn't good but I had to dig deep. So the early part of my life I was just fighting to be good enough and that's how I ended up in toxic relationships and friendships taking what I can get, giving too much too soon because I feared losing people.

Mental health illnesses and disorders are only going to expand and more things will be discovered and more issues with double diagnosis. The conversation have to continue from the household, school, books, television as much as we try to educate kids on safe sex we need to educate them about mental health. They need to understand how to treat people across the board no matter if they have an issue or not. Adults need to know the signs and symptoms so they can be aware when someone is going through something. Nowadays mental health is as common as a cold because so many households ignore or sweep issues under the rug thinking it will disappear.

Not addressing mental health only hurts us all in the long wrong. Let's take a child who grew up in a household where their father beat their mother; the abuse was never talked about combined with no counselling for the parents now the child's outlook on love could have been altered. This can lead to poor choices of men or women in the future and what they allow or endure they might not see it as a problem because it was normal in their household. Now you are a person who thinks that if you're not arguing or fighting it's not love, or that abuse is not bad. What if this person has kids of their own? You see how things can trickle down? Most of our behaviors are learned behaviors, and a person dealing with something for years is going to have issues. Abuse, rape, molestation, bullying, poverty, disability, even just looking different and feeling different are things depression, ptsd, and anxiety can come from and so much more. Some people have been through so much stuff they are immune to it, they think hey it's life. More people need hugs, a shoulder to cry on, a person to talk to, a professional to guide them and help them with certain thoughts and behaviors that run through their mind. Most of the strongest people you see out here are some of the most broken people.

I can't even process or accept compliments and I'm always hard on myself or think that I haven't done too much of anything. I had this mindset growing up and throughout some parts of my adult years. I simply believed I wasn't good enough. For me, talking about mental health is bigger than just opening up about myself, it's about opening doors for others to be their truest selves. I lost myself for years trying to fit myself into places I didn't belong. I failed to see how dope of a person I already was. My imperfections are a part of my story and so are yours. My mental health issues aren't my story-they are a part of my story. It feels so good to completely and fully love myself and I hope you, the reader, feel the same way about yourself.

If you are out here living in fear of completing something because you don't know if you can handle it or afraid you might get overwhelmed, still do it. Challenge yourself to do whatever it takes to reach your goals and follow your dreams. We have so many gifted people with talents the world needs and some of those people never share it. Don't be that person! Share your gift and take care of yourself. I look at it like this: if I'm going to deal with my PTSD for the rest of my life, I'm going to fight to do what I want and love for the rest of my life.

Think about it, how it looks to wake up every day trying to tackle your mental health just to put yourself in environments you really don't want to be. Now if you have to be or you have a plan that's one thing, but I'm not walking into a job I hate on top of having my own personal issues that's not going to work. You got to get creative and figure out ways to do what you love most of the time as much as you can control. Sometimes when I look back and see how I was carrying myself I can't believe who I was nor do I like it. I'm grateful for being in the place I'm at now to be able to look at the old me and not cry or be ashamed of who I was. I used to tell my story with knots in my stomach watching the facial expression of the person I was talking to thinking about how they now may look at me. I believe that I wouldn't want to be around me anymore. I worried about people not wanting to deal with me because I didn't feel strong, but really I was so much more stable and so much stronger than I thought I was. That's the thing: you're not weak, you're not a victim, you're not weird, and you're definitely not crazy. You are a human being with problems and feelings. You are not always going to be okay and that's okay.

I can't even begin to imagine life without being me, being free from the pressure to put on a face of bravery when I was a slave to society and its perception of a reality they know nothing about. I'm being called crazy by a person who stakes out their boyfriends house when he doesn't answer the phone only after 3 months of dating; a person who calls their ex 108 times in one day just to tell them how much they hate them; a person who fakes an illness to receive a check. Man oh man when you sit back and really look at the people who have the nerve to speak on other people's illness just smile because they don't know any better. They think they're normal in society's eyes but they are so blind and misguided they don't even know they are dealing with the same things you are dealing with just on a different level. Remember your mental illness and struggles you may have with it doesn't have to be a death sentence or a long lasting issue that drains you or stops you from living life. How you heal from your troubles is first dealing with them, and there are so many different ways to, there is no excuse not to help yourself.

Never let a bad day or days ruin your life. Don't allow a moment of trauma to become a lifetime of pain. Seek help. I can't stress this enough: Seek help. There is nothing wrong with needing help. Love yourself enough to help yourself. And if you don't love yourself, I suggest you start! Yes, it will take time and some self-evaluation. Everything is a process, but when you're out here undervaluing yourself, not understanding your worth, not putting yourself first, now you walk around bleeding on others that didn't even cut you.

Love is needed for self-first so it can properly be given to your family, friends, and lovers. You don't deserve to walk around handcuffing your pain internally, and people who are in your life don't deserve the effects of that pain or trauma you choose not to deal with. Man I hope I don't make it sound easy in this book getting help and digging deep to become a better you. I know it's hard; it took me a few years. I stopped and started on the journey to self-love, I got distracted, I got scared, I felt like nobody was going to be there when I fell because when you get to the core of your problems before you rise you will fall. The falling is not a bad thing it's just for instance when I started my journey seriously to get myself to write the layers of pain, discomfort, poor decision making, and how I was moving just the realization of it all it felt like a punch in the stomach. I cried seeing that the more I hid myself and my pain the more unstable and inconsistent I was becoming as a person. I did my family, friends, and whoever else I was around an injustice because, while they got a nice, loving me, I was deeply scared. I was always petrified of losing them and never fully honest of my mood swings.

Being free from burying yourself inside is like no other feeling. I want people to feel the way I feel today- comfortable in my own skin. My struggle with mental health hasn't disappeared, but it is better handled with proper care now that I no longer fear the whispers, stares, or opinions of others. You become a slave to your own troubles and for others they turn from victims to suspects if you know what I mean. I caused problems as well because of my fears of identifying with who I was. I made a lot of poor decisions, rash decisions that led to more problems on top of more problems. So yes, I basically caused some self-inflicted wounds not intentionally but due to being in denial and my lack of help.

None of us are exempt from the trials and tribulations that come with life. Disease and disorders don't pick and choose between whether they will affect rich or poor people. If you are reading this and my words are starting to get to you and make you think-take a deep breath. Realize that this is a sign for you to start to help yourself out. I'm not here to break you but I need for the people who are in denial or struggling to deal with mental health to understand these words I'm writing. I want my words to hit a nerve. I'll do whatever it takes for you to look at yourself differently in the mirror. It's a no-judgement zone over here and I'm sending all of the love and support I can muster to get you out of your own way. You are not weak because you are emotional or have issues. Your thought of weakness is your mind playing tricks on you. You don't have to open yourself up to the world like I am doing but you do have to talk to someone and begin to heal inside out. You got this! We got this! I am with you and millions of other people as well. Never lose faith. Never feel alone. And always remember; YOU'RE ILL!

NOTE TO SELF!

You cannot live with yourself if you don't love yourself.

You cannot heal yourself if you don't trust yourself.

You cannot wait for answers or even a cure.

You have to acknowledge, accept, and absorb the person you are and get on the journey to where you want to be.

You won't last in this world if your subconscious isn't free.

Free of negativity, self-doubt, and insecurity.

Free of hate, shame, and unloyalty.

Trust the progress and the road to self-discovery.

Trust in God and you'll see a recovery.

Within your mind and the way you live.

Your diagnosis depends on what you allow in your head.

There will be dark days ahead.

Days you feel like only lying in the bed.

But another day is another blessing to get back on your game.

Don't let your family, peers, and society only remember your diagnosis make them remember your name!

www.ingramcontent.com/pod-product-compliance
Lightning Source LLC
Chambersburg PA
CBHW050913160426
43194CB00011B/2390